Content

G000091346

Helping you Get an A Grade

Effective learning involves reducing difficult topics into smaller, "bite-sized" chunks.

Every revision guide, card or coursebook from PushMe Press comes with its own website consisting of summaries, handouts, games, model essays, revision notes and more. Each website community is supported by the best teachers in the country.

At the end of each chapter you will see an **i-pu-sh** web link that you can type into your web browser along with a QR code that can be scanned by our free app.

These links will give you immediate access to the additional resources you need to "Get an A Grade" by providing you with the relevant information needed.

Getting an A Grade has never been easier.

Download our FREE How to Get an A Grade in Ethics app for your phone or tablet and get up-to-date information that accompanies this book and the whole PushMe Press range.

http://ethics.pushmepress.com/download

SAMPLE ESSAYS

You need to understand the difference between AO1 (analytical) and AO2 (evaluative) criteria which are used in marking your exam. You will find a discussion of these exam marking criteria attached to marked sample essays by scanning this code. Teachers also have added suggestions on how to improve these real answers. Essays are arranged by syllabus theme.

http://i-pu.sh/G7J95D37

EXTENDING (ALPHA POINTS)

Some analytical or evaluative points raise the quality of your answers. We call these "extending" points (for example, making a connection with another idea or a different philosopher). For a list of such extending points by topic, you can scan this code.

http://i-pu.sh/J9B55H60

Introduction

I have spent most of my working life trying to get students A grades.

Of course, sometimes you don't succeed. But I have tried to encourage my students to apply these five principles, and I honestly believe that those who have done so have raised their chances considerably, and many have giving me a fantastic surprise, scoring way above my expectations.

But to do the analysis behind these five principles does take time - quite a lot of time, which I admit you may not have.

So in this book I've done it for you, using the OCR Philosophy and Ethics A level as my course. But you could apply the same steps to pretty much any exam board, and any subject, and if you do so, I think your prospects of A grade will be greatly enhanced.

- **PRINCIPLE 1** - Understand the philosophy behind your exam.

- **PRINCIPLE 2** - Do a close analysis of the exam syllabus.

- **PRINCIPLE 3** - Do a close analysis of past questions.

- **PRINCIPLE 4** - Do a close analysis of the relation between syllabus and questions.

- **PRINCIPLE 5** - Do a close analysis of the Chief Examiner's mark schemes and reports.

Finally, I include throughout the book some ideas on how to revise effectively, both as an individual and as a group, including a number of class revision exercises.

What are Exams for?

Is there a reason for exams, a philosophy behind the subject you are doing?

The answer is "yes" and it helps if you understand the philosophy behind Philosophy and Ethics, because in the end, if you become a philosopher and can show this in the exam, you should gain close to full marks.

The word philosophy means "a love of wisdom," and we gain wisdom by exercising a special type of thinking skill. The Greeks believed this skill was a foundational skill, because thinking well was a key to living well. So, we might ask, how do we "think well?"

I was encouraged recently to hear of a school which has a cookie club which meets at 4pm every week on a Thursday. The idea of the cookie club is to meet and debate - or if you like, to argue a case. Sometimes a member of staff and sometimes a pupil, comes with a case to defend, and everyone has to argue against the point of view that pupil is defending.

Something like this underlies the subject of philosophy. Philosophy is about presenting, arguing and then defending a case. So, for example, Plato uses a method of dispute in his writing, called the Socratic method, where he puts words into the mouth of an adversary and then proceeds to dispute and disprove that opponent's case.

Of course this begs some questions.

WHAT DO I ACTUALLY BELIEVE ABOUT, SAY, GAY MARRIAGE?

I awarded a prize recently to anyone who could provide a good philosophical case against gay marriage. I announced the prize at a conference, and I guess it was no surprise that the speaker next to me murmured "there isn't one."

The speaker is of course wrong. The problem is, we sometimes need moral courage to oppose a view which most people hold. If I (for the sake of argument) oppose gay marriage, some people might call me a homophobe; other people may describe me as a right-wing fundamentalist, out of tune with reality.

But philosophers should not worry about this. Because philosophy is concerned with the nature and strength of arguments and nothing else. People can cause me to take poison like Socrates had to, they can insult me in newspapers and they can walk out of conferences. But we need to hold steadfastly to this point: social welfare only proceeds by the analysis and evaluation of arguments. It is only by this process that any great social reform has come. Bad arguments produce bad politics and bad policies; good arguments do the opposite.

In your A level, have the courage to present and then own for yourself, good, strong, well-justified arguments and you will be on the way to an A grade.

WHAT MAKES AN ARGUMENT WEAK?

A weak argument can really only be of two types. It can be logically unsound. And it can be factually unsound. Some arguments may present both weaknesses.

For example, consider this argument:

1. The world is either flat or square.

2. The world is not flat.

3. So the world must be square.

What is wrong with this? Well, it is false in two senses. First it commits a logical mistake - of restricting the options. It only gives us a choice of two possibilities, flat or square, when in fact there are many possible shapes, and the correct answer (the world is round) isn't given as a possibility.

Secondly, it is empirically or factually false. As a matter of fact, if I set off in my little sailing boat and head west (assuming I remember to navigate for the Panama Canal) I will eventually end up where I started. So I can attack the argument on two grounds, the logical and the factual, making clear what my two grounds are.

What about this argument about abortion?

1. The foetus resembles a human being at eleven weeks.

2. Human beings have feelings, thoughts, and desires.

3. Therefore a foetus has feelings, thoughts and desires at eleven weeks.

What is wrong with this argument? It actually begs a question, or perhaps begs two questions: Is resembling a human being enough to infer that something is a human being? After all, statues, dolls and toy soldiers all resemble human beings. But that doesn't mean they are human beings.

Secondly, it lists a number of things that human beings do: they feel, think and want things. These may be necessary conditions for being human - it's hard to imagine a human being, except one in a persistent vegetative state, that doesn't at least have feelings. But is that list sufficient for defining a human being? After all my dog feels, thinks and wants its walk at 8am, but I wouldn't call my dog human.

Some facts are important for ethics. It is morally important where we can establish beyond doubt that the planet is warming. It is morally important whether a foetus feels pain (estimates range from 18 to 26 weeks) and at what stage of development. It is morally important in IVF treatment to know how many cycles a woman is allowed on the NHS and what the chances of success are - as these raise questions of rights and justice. Is it fair that my hospital excludes women over 37 from treatment? It is morally important to know who suffers when the company Trafigura dumps toxic waste in the Ivory Coast and how much compensation the inhabitants deserve for their suffering.

But, of course, we must check the facts. Bad facts produce bad ethics - and it wasn't long ago that some people were arguing that certain races were less intelligent than others, as a monstrous argument for discrimination, well considered in the recent film on President Lincoln.

WHAT MAKES AN ARGUMENT STRONG?

A strong argument proceeds by a logical form, from assumptions to conclusion. On the way, the argument requires analysis and, if the question demands it, evaluation. Many students don't understand the difference between analysis and evaluation, so perhaps we can clarify this.

Analysis means that an argument proceeds by a process of reasoning. When we reason we substantiate (back up) the argument. This means we give justifications for a particular viewpoint. For example, we say that Kant argues that morality is an "a priori" process of reasoning, because he sees the moral ought as applying universally, everywhere and for all time. If this is the case, then he argues we cannot be subject to the realm of emotions or peer group pressure, because this would make the moral ought conditional on what people think or feel at any particular time.

Notice that in this argument I use the word "because" a number of times. I spell out the reasons for my reasoning. I also use a hypothetical statement, which starts with "if" and then continues with "then." The "if" here is indicating an underlying assumption, that we can divide the world up into two realms of thinking, what Kant calls the noumenal world (of pure ideas) and the phenomenal world (of experiences that we feel, see, touch).

If I was evaluating Kant rather than giving a Kantian analysis, then I might question this assumption. Is it a good way of looking at the world? Can there really be a pure realm of ideas in themselves? How does this differ from the utilitarian view of the world, and is the utilitarian view superior? If so, why? If not, why not?

But notice that if the examiner is asking me just to explain the Kantian worldview (as will happen at AS level in part a of a question) then any evaluation is irrelevant. However, if we are asked to evaluate or even discuss Kant's worldview (as could happen at AS part b of a question, or at A2 level, where in OCR we are still expected to know about Kant and apply him to sexual ethics, for example) then such a discussion is certainly relevant.

WHAT MAKES AN ARGUMENT INTERESTING?

Believe it or not the examiner can get bored reading the same textbook-regurgitated material script after script. So we need to make our arguments interesting. There are two main ways of doing this:

Make your argument different

For example, where most candidates might be expected to approve of utilitarian ethics (as it's the dominant way of thinking ethically in our society), why not attack utilitarian ethics? We could take as our starting point Arthur Koestler's quote, that people, in the name of utilitarianism, "have visited upon the human race such terrible privations ..." and develop this idea. Our development might go like this: Governments claim to be arbiters of the common good. In imposing a decision on society, they can, for utilitarian reasons, ignore dissenters and the rights of those who are adversely affected. They can justify this in the name of progress and general welfare. Which is exactly what totalitarian governments have done. You could then connect this idea to Stalin's forced collectivisation which led to the deaths of over ten million Russians.

Make your examples real

Examiners like us to use examples which are up-to-date or personal. In order to do this, we could use a film to illustrate our argument. Imagine we are talking about virtue ethics. We could use the film Untouchable, which shows how an unemployed man caring for a wealthy disabled man in Paris would transform his life by relating to him as a human being with real needs and feelings, rather than as a category of "disabled." In this way the care worker shows that goodness isn't about rules (how I should care for people) but about character traits such as honesty, integrity, compassion and humour (one of Aristotle's key virtues).

Or we could take an example from our own experience. Should we ever save a stranger in distress? Has anyone ever saved you, or have you ever saved a stranger? What is the moral motivation for doing so? Is it a feeling (which seems to argue against Kant) or a sense of duty (which seems to argue for Kant's idea that we act on duty alone)?

Or we might use books we are reading, novels, biographies or everyday descriptions from books. The point is, make our essays interesting and show we can relate abstract ethics and philosophy to real life, and we will make an A grade much more likely. That's one way of producing A grade reflection.

HOW DO I PRACTISE STRENGTHENING ARGUMENTS?

I wrote a book last year with my colleague Brian Poxon called "How to Write Philosophy Essays." In that book we describe a technique for writing essays. Here's a brief description of how this technique works.

Imagine I have an A2 essay title like: "To what extent are ethical theories helpful when considering ethical business practice?" (OCR June 2012).

I need to practise presenting what we can call my thesis in the first line of the essay. The thesis is simply your statement of your line of reasoning on this particular question. For example:

- **THESIS** - "Ethical theories are useful to the extent that they prevent immoral outcomes - such as harm to the environment or exploitation of third world workers. Neither deontological nor teleological theories are immune from criticism, and here we assess to what extent their principles can be clearly and justly applied to business practices."

  This statement has the advantages of being unmistakably relevant to this exact question and also very clear.

- The second thing I can do is reduce every paragraph to a one sentence statement of the argument of that paragraph.

- **PARAGRAPH 1** - Explains how a Kantian deontologist might derive ethical principles and apply them to business practices such as the two mentioned above.

- **PARAGRAPH 2** - Applies this to a case study such as Trafigura, which dumped toxic waste on the Ivory Coast.

- **PARAGRAPH 3** - Explores how the utilitarianism of Mill might handle the same two issues.

- **PARAGRAPH 4** - Considers how utilitarian ethics might inform the Trafigura directors considering where to dump the waste, and also reveals the assumptions that they might make (which may be poor assumptions, such as that they would not be found out and sued). See the website for further information of this case.

- **CONCLUSION** - Both Kantian ethics and utilitarian ethics has problems in the derivation and application of clear moral principles. They are useful only in so far as a Kantian can universalise his or her behaviour imaginatively and give some ethical weight to environmental concerns. And utilitarianism is useful only in so far as it does not sue people as means to an end and can accurately forecast the consequences. Even then it has this problem: that you can get away with an action with damaging effects does not make it right.

So, try to sketch out a thesis, practise this technique, and then try saying something interesting, surprising even, which of course must be fully justified. Many questions need to be **NARROWED** in order to make the answer manageable. Here I have narrowed it to two instances of immoral outcomes and two theories presented as a contrast. This is how you maximise chances of an A grade.

WHY DO DEFINITIONS MATTER SO MUCH?

In Philosophy of Religion and Ethics there is technical vocabulary which must be used correctly. But we need to be aware that the task of philosophy is also to indicate ambiguities in key words, how they are used differently in different contexts and how the meaning is not necessarily clear-cut or fixed.

I was listening to a debate on Question Time recently and it became clear to me that two sides of this debate were actually talking about a different thing. The subject was gay marriage. On one side, the definition of marriage here meant something like: "a relationship where two people are fully committed to one another." No mention of sexual relations here.

On the other side, the definition was something like this: "marriage is a lifelong commitment between a man and a woman where heterosexual sex is the natural expression, and children the natural fruit, of such a lifelong commitment." Notice that this definition includes both sex and the possibility of children.

I think the chairman of this debate, David Dimbleby, should have pointed out that people were talking about two different things. The question is, which is the correct definition, or the most useful definition? Clearly the second is the traditional view of marriage, whereby not having sexual relations is a ground for divorce or annulment of the marriage. Once we have established we are talking about different things we can then decide what we think.

Does it matter that the definition of marriage is changing? Should marriage necessarily include some idea of sexual relations? If it doesn't, could I marry someone who remains my best friend, who I never even touch? If marriage includes some idea of sexual relations, how do we define sexual relations between two men?

All this helps to clarify the debate - and this is the task of philosophy. For philosophy has at its heart a philosophy of argument - of clarification, reasoning and conclusions which make sense. To argue effectively we cannot help defining and clarifying our terms and indicating possible ambiguities in their use. The examiner's reports, analysed in the final chapter, repeatedly emphasise a failure to grasp key terms is a major reason why candidates don't get A grades.

How to Analyse the Specification

Students can sometimes be surprised by questions set in the exam. However, there never should be any element of surprise, as the specifications (syllabuses) lay down exactly what you can expect in the exam. Therefore surprise can only come because there is an area of the specification we failed to notice, or failed to cover adequately. A grade technique involves:

- Examining the specification, paying close attention to specific authors mentioned.

- Relating past questions to the specification to see how the examiner interprets the specification, which may be ambiguous in places.

In this section we will analyse the four specifications, before matching the specification to past questions in a later chapter.

AS ETHICS (OCR G572)

Candidates should be able to demonstrate knowledge and understanding of:

- the concepts of absolutist and relativist morality;

- what it means to call an ethical theory absolutist and objective;

- what it means to call an ethical theory relativist and subjective;

- the terms deontological and teleological.

Candidates should be able to discuss critically these concepts and their strengths and weaknesses.

Ethical theories: Natural Law

Candidates should be able to demonstrate knowledge and understanding of:

- the origins of Aquinas' Natural Law in Aristotle's idea of purpose;

- Aquinas' ideas of purpose and perfection;

- the use of reason to discover Natural Law;

- the primary and secondary precepts.

Candidates should be able to discuss critically these views and their strengths and weaknesses.

Ethical theories: Kantian ethics

Candidates should be able to demonstrate knowledge and understanding of:

- the difference between the Categorical and the Hypothetical Imperatives;

- the various formulations of the Categorical Imperative;

- Kant's understanding of the universalisation of maxims;

- Kant's theory of duty;

- Kant's ideas of the moral law, good will and the summum bonum.

Candidates should be able to discuss critically these theories and their strengths and weaknesses.

Ethical theories: Utilitarianism

Candidates should be able to demonstrate knowledge and understanding of:

- the classical forms of Utilitarianism from Bentham and Mill;

- the principle of Utility;

- the differences between the Utilitarianism of Bentham and of Mill;

- the Hedonic Calculus, higher and lower pleasures, quantity vs quality, Act and Rule Utilitarianism;

- the Preference Utilitarianism of Peter Singer.

Candidates should be able to discuss critically these issues and their strengths and weaknesses.

Ethical theories: Religious ethics

Religious ethics - a study of the ethics of the religion chosen by the candidate.

Candidates should be able to demonstrate knowledge and understanding of:

- the main ethical principles of the religion studied and how the followers of the religion make ethical decisions;

- the ways in which religion and morality may seem to be linked or be seen as separate from each other;

- how far morality may be seen as dependent on God (Divine Command theory);

- how far religious ethics may be seen as absolutist or relativist;

- how ethical theories may be considered religious.

Candidates should be able to discuss critically these issues and their strengths and weaknesses.

Applied ethics

The ethical theories:

- Natural Law

- Kantian Ethics

- Utilitarianism

- Religious Ethics

as applied to the ethical topics below.

▶ Abortion: the right to a child

Candidates should be able to demonstrate knowledge and understanding of:

- the concept of the "sanctity of life" and how it applies to abortion;

- the concept of personhood as applied to abortion;

- the right to life as applied to abortion and the rights of all those involved;

- the issues of infertility and the right to a child;

- the status of the embryo;

- whether a child is a gift or a right;

- the application and the different approaches of the ethical theories listed above to abortion and the right to a child.

Candidates should be able to discuss critically these issues and their strengths and weaknesses.

▸ Euthanasia

Candidates should be able to demonstrate knowledge and understanding of:

- the concept of the "sanctity of life" and how it applies to euthanasia;

- the concept of the "quality of life" and how it applies to euthanasia;

- the right to life as applied to euthanasia;

- the application and the different approaches of the ethical theories listed above to euthanasia.

Candidates should be able to discuss critically these issues and their strengths and weaknesses.

▸ Genetic engineering

Candidates should be able to demonstrate knowledge and understanding of:

- the ethical questions raised by the different types of genetic engineering to humans, animals and plants; human embryo research;

- the application and the different approaches of the ethical theories listed above to genetic engineering.

Candidates should be able to discuss critically these issues and their strengths and weaknesses.

▸ War and peace

Candidates should be able to demonstrate knowledge and understanding of:

- the principles of 'Just War' and its application;

- the theories of ethical and religious pacifism;

- the application and the different approaches of the ethical theories listed above to war and peace.

Candidates should be able to discuss critically these issues and their strengths and weaknesses.

Technical language in the syllabus

As we read through these specifications some general points seem to stand out. The first is that the specification helpfully breaks each topic up into subheadings. The second is that these subheadings contain specific technical language. The examiner has listed the technical language which, as a minimum, we are expected to use, and which we might expect to appear in the questions set.

So what is the technical language? You could take this opportunity to tick off the ones you can define easily without looking up.

Technical language at Ethics AS level includes:

- Absolute
- Relative
- Subjective
- Objective
- Deontological
- Teleological
- Natural Law
- Primary precepts
- Secondary precepts
- Categorical Imperative
- Hypothetical Imperative
- Duty
- Summum bonum
- Act Utilitarianism
- Rule Utilitarianism
- Principle of utility
- Hedonic calculus
- Qualitative pleasures
- Preference Utilitarianism
- Personhood (the embryo)
- Sanctity of Life
- Right to a child
- Quality of Life (euthanasia)
- Just War
- Ethical pacifism
- Religious pacifism

Now this is a minimum list - there are more technical terms we might want to use in an essay - but we should start with this list and make sure we understand exactly what these terms mean and indeed, what the alternative interpretations of their meanings might be. For example, the term "sanctity of life" has a different meaning to a Kantian than it does to a Roman Catholic. To a Kantian, it means "never treating a human being as just a means to an end, but always also as an end in themselves." Of course, this begs the question of whether the embryo should be classed as a human being. But to a Roman Catholic "sanctity of life" means "designed and created by God with absolute value" which includes embryonic life, as life begins at conception.

In the past I can think of two examples of questions which surprised students, but really should not have done. The examiner has asked the part a AS question: "Explain Peter Singer's Preference Utilitarianism" which is dealt with very inadequately by textbooks and which teachers often gloss over altogether. The part b asked us to consider whether Preference Utilitarianism was the best form. These questions are quite challenging, but not unfair or surprising.

Secondly, the examiner has asked us the question: "Distinguish between ethical and religious pacifism." This again is clearly specified in the syllabus, so should come as no surprise. Yet students were often ill-prepared for this question, failing to see that much Just War theory is coming from religious tradition (be it Catholic or Islamic), and so ethical pacifism is a different, if related, idea. Indeed the phrase "ethical pacifism" is ambiguous as surely religious pacifism is ethical pacifism of one sort? A good answer might consider this, whilst also going on to explain, for example, a Kantian approach to pacifism as contained in his Essay on Perpetual Peace, or the view of the atheist Bertrand Russell who became a conscientious objector to the first World War.

Authors mentioned

The following authors are mentioned, and although the syllabus makes clear you are not expected to read original sources, I believe the A grade candidate will want to read these authors for themselves. Extracts are available on the website. There are no specific authors mentioned for the applied ethics side of the specification: a good student will however draw up their own list of authors who address issues raised by the specification.

- Aquinas
- Aristotle
- Kant
- Bentham
- Mill
- Singer

Critical discussion

You will have noticed that the phrase "candidates should be able to discuss critically these issues and their strengths and weaknesses" occurs again and again. We need to be able to discuss the issues critically. What might this phrase mean?

Firstly, as I mentioned above, we need to understand how Kant, Mill, Singer or Aquinas arrive at their conclusions. As they move from analysis to conclusion do they make any moves which we might consider are errors? And what are their starting points or assumptions?

Before we go any further we need to be clear that in part a AS questions we are never expected to evaluate - in other words, we will never be asked to assess critically Kant's Categorical Imperative, or Aquinas' idea of rational purpose. However we might be asked to "Explain the major weaknesses of Kant's ethical theory," which sounds like evaluation but is actually analysis.

I would suggest two ways of preparing for this aspect of the syllabus. When we look at each theory, it is important to ask what the starting point or assumptions are, and to do this, we need to understand the worldview which the philosopher is coming from. In the table below I summarise how assumptions and worldview interact in the major ethical theories which we encounter at AS and A2.

THEORY	ASSUMPTIONS	OBJECTIONS
Relativism	*There is no universal truth*	*May be empirically false*
Natural Law	*Humans by nature do good*	*Humans by nature are selfish and do more evil than good*
Kantian Ethics	*Reason is divided between the noumenal and phenomenal realms, and morality belongs to the noumenal*	*Moral principles seem to be derived by many philosophers from the natural or empirical world eg by adding up happiness*
Utilitarianism - Bentham	*Pleasure is the only good* *We can measure pleasure*	*There seem to be other "goods" such as duty* *We can't measure pleasure in hedons or anything else*
Divine Command	*God's word is clear and unambiguous on practical issues*	*Ancient texts were written from one cultural perspective which often does not address our culture directly*
Utilitarianism - Mill	*There are higher and lower pleasures* *Rules are needed to maximise utility*	*This is a difficult distinction to make without sounding snobbish* *Rules imply universal application - so when can you break them?*
Virtue Ethics	*A virtue is an agreed character trait. This trait comes from the rational purpose (telos) of human beings*	*We cannot agree on whether things like courage are really a moral virtue. What about the kamikaze pilot?*

Secondly, I think we should all draw up tables of strengths and weaknesses, at least for the ethical theories in question. This is the approach I take on the website where you can find examples of such tables under each section. But when you do this, make sure you link counteracting views with a philosopher and preferably, a quote from a philosopher. Learn some of these evaluative quotes for the exam, as they give you ideas which you can develop in the substance of your own essays. The extracts in each section (listed as Extract 1, Extract 2 etc) are also presented in each section on the website to help you extract key quotes and ideas from philosophers both dead and alive, so that your essays can gain more weight and a sense of engagement with ideas.

At A2 OCR the part a and part b format disappears, and so we expect to do the analysis and evaluation in one continuous thread of argument. Indeed this is the best approach, as the examiner has hinted that tagging evaluation on at the end weakens the essay.

A2 ETHICS (OCR G582)

Ethical topics and theories: Meta-ethics

Candidates should be able to demonstrate knowledge and understanding of:

- The use of ethical language - the ways in which different scholars understand how words like "good," "bad," "right," "wrong" are used when ethical statements are made;

- How meta-ethics differs from normative ethics;

- The different approaches: cognitive and non-cognitive; ethical naturalism, intuitionism; emotivism and prescriptivism and how these apply to ethical statements.

Candidates should be able to discuss these areas critically and their strengths and weaknesses.

Ethical topics and theories: Free will and determinism

Candidates should be able to demonstrate knowledge and understanding of:

- Hard determinism, soft determinism and libertarianism;

- The views of Darrow, Honderich, Hume and Locke;

- Theological determinism (predestination) and religious ideas of free will;

- The influences of genetics, psychology, environment or social conditioning on moral choices;

- The implications of these views for moral responsibility;

- The link between free will, determinism and moral responsibility.

Candidates should be able to discuss these areas critically and their strengths and weaknesses.

Ethical topics and theories: Nature and role of the conscience

Candidates should be able to demonstrate knowledge and understanding of:

- The different views of the conscience as God-given, innate or the voice of reason or instilled by society, parents, authority figures;

- Whether conscience is a reliable guide to ethical decision-making;

- The views of Augustine, Aquinas, Butler, Newman, Freud, Fromm, Piaget.

Candidates should be able to discuss these views critically and their strengths and weaknesses.

Ethical topics and theories: Virtue ethics

Candidates should be able to demonstrate knowledge and understanding of:

- The principles of Virtue Ethics from Aristotle;

- The 'agent-centred' nature of Virtue Ethics;

- The concepts of eudaimonia and the Golden Mean;

- The importance of practising the virtues and the example of virtuous people;

- More modern approaches to Virtue Ethics.

Candidates should be able to discuss these areas critically and their strengths and weaknesses.

Applied ethics

The ethical theories:
- Natural Law
- Kantian Ethics
- Utilitarianism
- Religious Ethics
- Virtue Ethics

as applied to all the applied ethics topics listed below.

Environmental and Business ethics

Candidates should be able to demonstrate knowledge and understanding of:

- The issue of how humans should relate to the environment, its resources and species;

- Secular approaches - the Gaia hypothesis;

- Issues in business ethics: the relationship between business and consumers; the relationship between employers and employees; the relationship between business and the environment; business and globalisation; the application and the different approaches of the ethical theories listed above to environmental and business ethics.

Candidates should be able to discuss these areas critically.

Sexual ethics

Candidates should be able to demonstrate knowledge and understanding of:

- The issues surrounding sexual ethics - premarital and extramarital sex, contraception and homosexuality;

- The application and the different approaches of the ethical theories listed above to sexual ethics;

Candidates should be able to discuss these areas critically.

At A2 two areas have produced particular problems for students. The first is Meta-ethics or theories of ethical meaning. This produces difficulties because of the sheer weight of technical vocabulary (see list below). And it appears to be a little obscure why so many theories of the meaning of good are actually required.

But many philosophers would argue that meta-ethics is foundational to the subject as, remembering the discussion of the word marriage above; if we don't know exactly what we are talking about when we use the word "good" then we can find ourselves talking past one another. In fact today we live in an era of the resurgence of ethical naturalism, the view that ethical ideas have grounding in features of the natural world. This movement is led by philosophers like the virtue ethicist Alasdair MacIntyre, who wholeheartedly rejects the so-called naturalistic fallacy, and sees ethics grounded in a common idea of welfare derived from both the Bible and science.

The second area of difficulty comes with the introduction of environmental and business ethics into the syllabus. Teachers have been unsure how to handle this topic, and indeed, it does seem like two areas curiously conflated. Again, there is technical vocabulary to learn and some clarification to pursue as to how to use an idea like globalisation productively in an essay on ethics.

Technical vocabulary

Adopting the same approach we did at AS, it is best to list all the technical terms mentioned in the syllabus, and then make sure we have also noted all the specific authors mentioned so that we have something to say about each of them. The technical vocabulary relating to the ethical theories at AS still apply, as Natural Law, Kant, Utilitarianism and Religious ethical theories will need to be applied to environment and business ethics and sexual ethics (the theory of virtue ethics is added to these theories at A2).

- Naturalism
- Cognitivism
- Non-cognitivism
- Prescriptivism
- Emotivism
- Intuitionism
- Hard determinism
- Soft determinism (compatibilism)
- Libertarianism
- Agent-centred virtue ethics
- Eudaimonia
- Golden Mean
- Gaia hypothesis
- Globalisation
- Extramarital sex
- Contraception
- Homosexuality

Again, it needs to be stressed that this is a minimum list of those terms mentioned specifically in the A2 syllabus. Past experience, however, suggests that these are the very terms which may appear in the exam question, and if they are not fully understood it will be impossible for candidates to answer these questions adequately. So learn them, understand them and know some of the possible variations of understanding of these terms. Major textbooks usually contain a glossary of key terms, but a word of warning: the way these definitions are reduced to one line means they lack nuance and may even be guilty of gross and misleading generalisations.

Authors mentioned

It is interesting just how many authors are specifically mentioned in the A2 ethics syllabus. This is important as the examiner may name one of them in the exam question and if you are underprepared on that one author you will be unable to do the question justice. So, again, I list them here for you to use as a checklist. I have listed these exactly in the order they come in the syllabus, so if you're in doubt which section a name refers to, then refer back to the syllabus.

- Darrow
- Honderich
- Hume
- Locke
- Augustine
- Aquinas
- Butler
- Newman
- Freud
- Fromm
- Piaget
- Aristotle

Again we need to stress this is a minimum list. For example, there are no philosophers mentioned in the Meta-ethics section of the syllabus so you will not be required to answer a question asking you to evaluate Alfred Ayer's view of goodness. But each of the theories mentioned, emotivism, prescriptivism, intuitionism have particular philosophers attached to them, so clearly underlying this section there are a number of names (Ayer, Hume, Hare, Moore, Ross, for instance).

Also, when we consider Virtue ethics, the examiner has made clear that answers simply dwelling on Aristotle (even though he is mentioned specifically in the syllabus) will not gain an A grade. So you or your teacher need to decide which of the modern virtue ethicists you intend to study in depth in order to fulfil that part of the syllabus asking us to consider modern virtue ethics (MacIntyre, Foot, Warnock, Slote, Louden for example).

Critical discussion

The A2 Ethics syllabus has left student and teacher with work to do filling in the gaps and interpreting how much additional content to supply. This comment particularly applies to three of the five sections: meta-ethics, virtue ethics and business and the environment.

However, we can be reasonably certain that the examiner wants us to contrast different views and then to decide, with justifications, which view we side with. This seems to be implicit in the command words "Discuss" or "Evaluate."

One way to prepare for the exam is to decide beforehand what your conclusion would be for any question the examiner might ask. For example, if we are asked to evaluate emotivism or prescriptivism or intuitionism it helps to have decided beforehand which theory we would side with, and why? What are the strengths and weaknesses of each? It is poor exam preparation to go into a paper unsure of your basic position.

So imagine we have the classic question: "Goodness is merely an expression of personal feelings." Discuss. Underlying this question is the argument for or against emotivism. Suppose that we have decided that we quite like emotivism as a theory and thus wish to defend this assertion (whilst also considering objections to it, of course).

I would then pre-prepare the following case: "Emotivism is the best explanation of the meaning of goodness because it recognises that the core element in statements of right and wrong is not reason, but feeling, and that no naturalistic explanation of the meaning of goodness escapes the naturalistic fallacy." I can then research some other authors, extract some quotes and make my own summary sheet around this base position - which could be adapted for another question such as: "Intuitionism is the best theory of the meaning of goodness." Discuss. You could then disagree with it by using the same justification of emotivism as a counter-argument.

Similarly, when we consider Virtue Ethics, students are frequently unable to compare and contrast Aristotle and MacIntyre, the ancient and modern views of Virtue Ethics. How do they differ? In what ways do they agree? I need to prepare my basic position, whether I am to side with MacIntyre's version or Aristotle's. If I prefer Aristotle, I must be able and willing to defend the Greek worldview that sees everything as having a purpose which is fulfilled according to some idea of perfection.

Finally, with environmental and business ethics it is probably fair to say that these two topics are just lumped together without much forethought as to how we should handle them. But that is no excuse for not mapping the territory clearly. Where there is inadequate structure in a syllabus, we must impose our own map to make sense of it. I do this on the website by drawing some diagrams elucidating the difference between ideas of intrinsic and instrumental goodness - as Gaia theory argues that the environment is intrinsically good (but what does that mean exactly?) whereas Utilitarian and Kantian ethics can only see the environment as instrumentally good - utilitarianism because there is one sole good, human happiness, or possibly the welfare of all sentient beings, and Kant only considers ethics from the standpoint of rational beings.

How to Analyse Past Exam Questions

Past exam questions give us critical clues as to how the examiner interprets the specification. As indicated in the previous chapter, the specification is ambiguous in several areas, and open to interpretation. What is certain is that no technical terms or authors will be mentioned in an exam question which isn't already mentioned in the syllabus.

The best approach to maximising A grade potential is to study carefully the trends in the questions, to examine which have been set before, and then relate them to the syllabus. Any areas that have never been examined before, or not for some time, are more likely to occur in the next paper set, as examiners have to range their questions across the whole syllabus and not stick to areas that may be easier to set questions on.

On the table below I have indicated the broad topic area by a cross. The exact wording of the questions is found in chapter 4 under the relevant syllabus section. Some crosses appear twice because questions may have an applied issue and a theory mentioned in the same question. This book is also revised every six months to bring the questions up to date, so it may be worth buying the latest edition.

AS ETHICS (OCR G572)

Categories

The following questions follow the syllabus areas. Notice that some questions, particularly those containing an application to one of the issues listed (abortion, euthanasia, war and peace or genetic engineering) cross over two columns. For example, one part a question from May 2011 reads: "explain theories of ethical and religious pacifism." This crosses over the theoretical aspect of religious ethics and the theories of war and peace. In fact Just War theory comes out of the religious tradition, hence the overlap.

However, not all applied ethics questions have a mention of an ethical theory or theories. Two part a questions from May 2012 simply state: "Explain the issues surrounding euthanasia/right to a child." The expectation here is that the student mentions at least one or two of the theories studied, but the question itself gives no requirement as to which theories. You would be unwise just to mention issues such as sanctity of life, quality of life, individual rights (to name some issues surrounding euthanasia) without relating them to ethical theories. A word of warning though, the examiner comments in the report on this question: "Many candidates used ethical theories to draw out moral issues and some were very successful in doing so, however, this approach to the question often meant that candidates missed the moral issues surrounding the right to a child and instead gave a general explanation of how the theories might approach the issue." It would be easy to fall into the trap of giving a simple GCSE style answer to this question which lacks depth or theoretical grounding, yet it is also easy to fall into the trap of answering a different question.

Spot the gaps

If I was predicting which topic areas might come up in June 2014, I would pay close attention particularly to areas which have not been examined recently such as Natural Law and Relativist Morality for AS and a less obvious aspect of Sexual Ethics (applied to any theory) for A2. This isn't to suggest you neglect other areas, but simply to highlight that certain topic areas are more likely to come up if they haven't been examined on for some time.

	Absolute/ Relative	Utilitarianism	Natural Law	Kant	Religious Ethics
Jan 2010	a. Explain what is meant by moral absolutism. b. "Moral absolutism cannot be justified." Discuss. *(1)*	a. Explain how utilitarians approach the issues of war. b. "Pacifism does more harm than good." Discuss. *(1)*	a. Explain the strengths of Natural Law Theory. b. To what extent could a follower of natural law accept embryo research? *(1)*	a. Explain the strengths of Natural Law Theory.	a. Explain how the ethics of a religion you have studied might be applied to abortion. b. "Religious ethics fail to consider consequences." Discuss. *(1)*
June 2010	a. Explain the differences between absolute and relative morality. b. "Relativist theories give no convincing reasons why people should be good." Discuss *(2)*	a. Explain the main strengths of Mill's Utilitarianism. b. Utilitarianism can lead to wrong moral decisions." Discuss. *(2)*		a. Explain how the followers of Kantian ethics might approach the issues surrounding the right to a child. b. "The right to a child is an absolute right." Discuss. *(1)*	a. Explain the ethical principles of a religion you have studied in relation to war. b. "War should not be allowed even as a last resort." Discuss. *(2)*
Jan 2011	a. Explain how a moral relativist might approach issues raised by abortion. b. "A relativist approach to issues raised by abortion leads to wrong moral decisions." Discuss. *(3)*	a. Explain the difference between Act and Rule Utilitarianism. b. To what extent is Utilitarianism a useful method of making decisions about euthanasia? *(3)*		a. Explain Kant's argument for using the Categorical Imperative. b. "The universalisation of maxims by Kant cannot be defended." Discuss. *(2)*	a. Explain how the followers of the ethics of a religion you have studied make ethical decisions. b. "Morality and religion are separate." Discuss. *(3)*
May 2011		a. Explain the Preference Utilitarianism of Peter Singer. b. To what extent is Preference Utilitarianism the best form of Utilitarianism? *(4)*	a. Explain the difference between the hypothetical and Categorical Imperative. b. How useful is Kant's theory when considering embryo research?	a. See Just War question *(3)*	

a) Explain how a follower of NL might approach abortion

b) 'Nat Law' has no serious weakness

(2)

	Abortion	Euthanasia	Just War	Right to a Child	Genetic Engineering
Jan 2010	See relgious ethics question a		See utilitarianism questions a & b	See natural law question b	
	(1)		(1)	(1)	
June 2010			see religious ethics questions a & b	See Kantian questions a & b	
			(2)	(2)	
Jan 2011	see relativism questions a & b	see utilitarianism question part b			
	(2)	(1)			
May 2011	N L (5)		a. Explain theories of ethical and religious pacifism b. Assess the claim that killing in war is more justifiable than other types of killing. (3)	see Kant question b (1)	

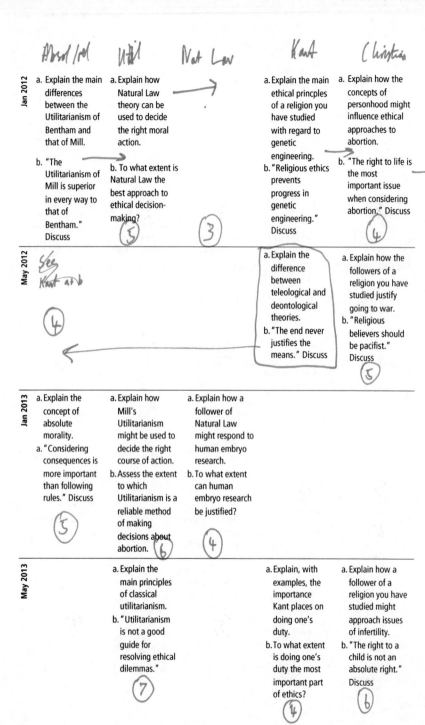

Handwritten column headers: Abor/ied · Util · Nat Law · Kant · Christian

Jan 2012	a. Explain the main differences between the Utilitarianism of Bentham and that of Mill. b. "The Utilitarianism of Mill is superior in every way to that of Bentham." Discuss	a. Explain how Natural Law theory can be used to decide the right moral action. b. To what extent is Natural Law the best approach to ethical decision-making? ⑤	③	a. Explain the main ethical princples of a religion you have studied with regard to genetic engineering. b. "Religious ethics prevents progress in genetic engineering." Discuss	a. Explain how the concepts of personhood might influence ethical approaches to abortion. b. "The right to life is the most important issue when considering abortion." Discuss ④
May 2012	*See Kant a + b* ④			a. Explain the difference between teleological and deontological theories. b. "The end never justifies the means." Discuss	a. Explain how the followers of a religion you have studied justify going to war. b. "Religious believers should be pacifist." Discuss ⑤
Jan 2013	a. Explain the concept of absolute morality. a. "Considering consequences is more important than following rules." Discuss ⑤	a. Explain how Mill's Utilitarianism might be used to decide the right course of action. b. Assess the extent to which Utilitarianism is a reliable method of making decisions about abortion. ⑥	a. Explain how a follower of Natural Law might respond to human embryo research. b. To what extent can human embryo research be justified? ④		
May 2013		a. Explain the main principles of classical utilitarianism. b. "Utilitarianism is not a good guide for resolving ethical dilemmas." ⑦		a. Explain, with examples, the importance Kant places on doing one's duty. b. To what extent is doing one's duty the most important part of ethics? ④	a. Explain how a follower of a religion you have studied might approach issues of infertility. b. "The right to a child is not an absolute right." Discuss ⑥

48

Abortion   Euthanasia   JW   Right to child   G.E

	Abortion	Euthanasia	JW	Right to child	G.E
Jan 2012					See religious ethics parts a and b ←
	→	③	②	③	
May 2012		a. a. Explain the moral issues surrounding euthanasia. b. "Quality of life is the most important factor when considering issues surrounding euthanasia." Discuss ③	a. See religious ethics question a. and b. ④	a. a Explain the moral issues surrounding the right to a child. b. "A child is a gift not a right." Discuss. ④	
Jan 2013	U til ④		a. Explain the purpose and principles of Just War theory. b. "Just War theory cannot be applied to modern warfare." Discuss ⑤		Nat Law ②
May 2013		a. Explain how the concept of 'Quality of Life' might be applied to euthanasia. b. "The Sanctity of Life is the most important issue when considering euthanasia." Discuss ④		a. See Religious ethics part a. and b. ⑤	

49

The wording of the questions

Exam questions either examine a theory listed in the syllabus, or an applied issue, or they combine the two, with a specific theory (Utilitarianism or Natural Law, for example, combined with pacifism).

Exam questions which ask you to explain a theory seem to follow a pattern.

1. Questions that ask you to explain some aspect of a theory. For example, you might be asked to explain Kant's Categorical Imperative, or Kant's idea of universalising moral precepts. You might be asked to explain Bentham's Hedonic calculus, or Aquinas' idea of Natural Law as it relates to human purpose. Remember that the thing you're being asked to explain is always mentioned in the syllabus: you may be asked to explain the Summum Bonum in Kant, but not the idea of the Noumenal realm in Kant.

2. Questions asking you to compare and contrast two theories or two aspects of the same general theory. For example, you might be asked to compare the Utilitarianism of Mill and Bentham, or explain the difference between a categorical and hypothetical imperative. You might be asked to explain the difference between a Natural Law and Kantian approach to explaining what is good, or between a teleological and deontological approach to deriving moral precepts. Finally, the difference between absolute and relative morality is an old favourite, so how about a question that asks you to explain the difference between absolute and relative approaches to moral decision-making?

3. Questions linking a theory to an application. These tend to follow the same wording. "Explain how a follower of Kant might approach issues surrounding abortion" or "Explain how a Natural Law theorist might justify going to war."

4. Finally, be wary of a trick the examiner sometimes plays. I have stressed that the word "evaluate" only applies to part b questions. In other words, in part a questions you will only be asked to explain something for the 25 marks on offer out of 35. But how about the question: "Explain the strengths of natural law theory?" Or "Explain the major weaknesses of utilitarian ethics?" You need to prepare to explain strengths and weaknesses as well as evaluate them (where evaluate here means say which you think are more or less valid strengths and weaknesses, and why?)

- **REVISION TIP** - Make up your own exam questions using the type of wording mentioned above, for areas that the examiner has not yet asked about. You can use oft-repeated phrases like "issues surrounding."

Questions which only mention an application such as the right to a child in part a, though unusual, are possible (there were two in the May 2012 paper). Here the technique is to clearly define the issues surrounding that applied area. So as a student you should prepare very thoroughly the issues surrounding abortion, euthanasia, the right to a child, genetic engineering, and war and peace. Try to identify at least three.

- **REVISION TIP** - Prepare a grid with the issues on one axis and the major theories on the other. Fill in the squares with some key points, for example, on how a Kantian interprets the sanctity of human life with abortion or euthanasia, using the second formulation of the Categorical Imperative: "never use people just as a means to an end, but always, also as an end in themselves." You can then compare this with a Natural Law view of sanctity of human life and consider whether sanctity of life is possible when related to utilitarian ethics.

Part b questions

Part b questions tend to be harder as they include evaluation, and they are demanding because you only have 10-15 minutes to complete your answer (which is only worth 10/35 marks and so really needs to be concise to gain full marks). Many candidates spend too little time on part a (describing rather than explaining) and too much time on part b.

There is no time to waste on neat opening paragraphs as you must go straight to the heart of the issue. I would prepare by drawing up my own strengths and weaknesses tables and learning one or two quotes from key philosophers for each. I would also complete a sentence which started "the advantages of utilitarian ethics are ... because ..." and trying to work out what my view is about the different theories. If you are evaluating you need to have a view which you can defend in a brief argument. The examiner continually stresses the need for evidence of **REFLECTION**.

- **REVISION TIP** - One minute debates are useful here. The teacher arranges chairs or desks in a circle with some students inside and some outside. The teacher then pre-prepares (or gets the class to pre-prepare) some "Discuss" questions. Then the students argue the case, the inner circle taking one view and the outer circle another (for and against the proposition). After one minute the whistle blows and the inner circle moves on one place.

When the debate has been had four or five times, a plenary session can be held where we construct together the strongest case on either side. Then the students can vote on which side they prepare. Finally each student can be asked to write a paragraph justifying their view - which must have reasons to back the view up. A prize could awarded for the most analytical answer.

A2 ETHICS (OCR G582)

There are five broad areas in the A2 syllabus for Ethics. But we should note that ethical theories studied at AS level, of Natural Law, Kant, Utilitarianism (in its three forms), and Religious Ethics can still feature in exam questions (and have been specifically named three times). The examiner also mentions "ethical theories" as a general term, which invites you to choose which you think are strong and which weak on any issue. It's worth preparing your (carefully reasoned) view on this: do you prefer Virtue Ethics or Kant, for example?

	Meta-ethics	Free Will ✓	Conscience ✓
Jan 2010	To what extent is ethical language meaningful?		Assess the view that conscience need not always be obeyed.
June 2010		Critically assess the claim that people are free to make moral decisions	
Jan 2011		"Our ethical decisions are merely the result of social conditioning." Discuss	Critically assess the claim that conscience is the voice of reason.
June 2011	"Ethical statements are no more than expressions of emotion." Discuss	Critically assess the view that we are not responsible for our evil actions.	
Jan 2012	"All ethical language is prescriptive." Discuss	Critically assess the claim that free will and determinism are compatible.	See sexual ethics question.
June 2012	To what extent do moral statements have objective meaning?		How convincing are Butler's claims that people have an innate sense of right and wrong?
Jan 2013			Critically assess the claim that conscience is a reliable guide to ethical decision-making.
June 2013	Critically assess the view that the word 'good' has no real meaning.	"Without freedom it is impossible to make moral choices." Discuss	

✓   ✓

	Virtue	Env and Bus ✓	Sexual Ethics ✓
Jan 2010		"Utilitarianism is not the best approach to environmental issues." Discuss **EE**	"Some ethical theories are more useful than others when making decisions about sexual ethics." Discuss
June 2010	"The weakness of virtue ethics outweigh its strengths." Discuss	Assess the usefulness of Religious Ethics as an ethical approach to business. **BE**	To what extent are ethical theories helpful when considering the issues surrounding homosexuality?
Jan 2011		"The environment suffers because business has no ethics." Discuss **BE/EE**	"Natural law is the most reliable approach when making decisions about pre-marital sex." Discuss
June 2011	To what extent is Virtue Ethics helpful when making decisions about extramarital sex? **SE**	Assess the claim that secular approaches to environmental issues are of more help than religious approaches. **EE**	
Jan 2012	To what extent do modern versions of Virtue Ethics address the weaknesses of Aristotle's teaching?		"For moral issues surrounding sex the demands of conscience override other ethical considerations." Discuss
June 2012		"There is no moral imperative to care for the environment." Discuss **EE** To what extent are ethical theories helpful when considering ethical business practice? **BE NOT**	
Jan 2013	"Following the example of virtuous people is the most useful aspect of Virtue Ethics." Discuss	Critically assess the view that businesses have a moral duty to put their consumers first. **BE**	"Religious approaches to sexual ethics are more helpful than secular approaches." Discuss
June 2013	"Businesses are completely incompatible with virtue ethics." Discuss. **BE**	To what extent are religious teachings on the environment and the Gaia hypothesis compatible? **EE**	

✓ BE ✓

Spot the gaps

Where one area is completely missed out in one paper it is usually examined in some form in the next paper set. But a thorough analysis of the specification also tells us that some themes in the syllabus have never been examined. This makes them more likely the longer they stay absent. For example, the issue of contraception has never featured in an exam question. There are also particular slants on a familiar topic area which have never been examined. Go to the next chapter to find out what they are.

Students often ask me if they can safely leave a topic area out altogether (the least favourite one being Meta-ethics). The answer is probably "yes" to this, as long as the strategies for handling any topic area suggested in this book are followed. Leave out Meta-ethics (for example) and you will still have three questions to choose from as long as the examiner doesn't repeat what happened in June 2012 - where two questions were set on the one syllabus area "environmental and business ethics."

Having said that: if you can master Meta-ethics, the questions are really quite predictable, and usually revolve around a core issue - which theory best makes sense of ethical statements. You can attack emotivism fairly hard as few people these days see much validity in AJ Ayer's view, whereas a theory like Prescriptivism would seem to be truer to how we use moral language. Remember too that naturalism (the objective basis for ethical statements) has made a comeback and so an answer defending naturalism against the naturalistic fallacy attack makes for an interesting essay which will stand out in this less popular topic area.

Wording of the questions

"Critically assess" and "assess" are favourite command words, also "to what extent," and a deliberately slanted comment followed by "Discuss." Essentially the technique is the same: to analyse theories and applications in a logical way and to point out strengths and weaknesses in a position as you go along. Unlike AS level, where part a questions ask you to explain something and part b to evaluate, here the evaluation and analysis should be woven together. Some ideas of how you can practise this for an exam are given in the final chapter of the book.

Ambiguities

My own view is that the Environmental and Business Ethics section is the least well thought out, and this perhaps explains why it hasn't been a popular area for examiners in the past. Part of the difficulty is that we have two areas of ethics which traditionally are dealt with separately and here they are placed together. There are linkages, of course. "The environment suffers because business has no ethics" might well be the view of many people. I prefer to teach this area looking at case studies of poor business practice and then applying a Kantian/Natural Law/Utilitarian/Virtue Ethics approach to issues that emerge. A core issue here is whether any ethical theory really addresses environmental issues, or whether we have to take refuge in the metaphysics of Gaia to make sense of the innate value of the environment.

Revision tip: Use real examples from the newspapers which are provided by our website or from your own research. There are some good films based on real life events, such as Erin Brockovich and the Constant Gardener. Recent cases include Glencore and Trafigura. Try to establish the motive of managers in these cases, and whether a study of ethical theories would have helped them.

How to Bring Specification and Past Questions Together

The specification gives an outline of the topics examined, and the subdivisions within the specification tell us which "twists" (as I call them) to expect. By lining up past questions against the specification we also get a clearer idea how to interpret the specification, and hence this allows us to predict more accurately questions in the future.

In this chapter we will break the specification down into sub-units and then match questions to each subdivision. Possible future questions are indicated by a star, past questions already set, by a tick.

In the table in the previous chapter I have indicated those broad syllabus areas examined in these two papers with a cross, so you can more easily spot the gaps. More gaps indicate higher probability and now we combine this with the idea of "examining the twists" which have not been given yet to a question or a syllabus theme.

AS ETHICS (OCR G572)

In this section we relate past questions (with the date set) to the specification and then consider which areas have not been examined on before. Possible future questions are marked below.

General terms

▸ **Absolute and relative**

Jan 2010 (a & b)

✓ Explain what is meant by moral absolutism.

✓ "Moral absolutism cannot be justified." Discuss.

June 2010 (a & b)

✓ Explain the differences between absolute and relative morality.

✓ "Relativism can give no convincing reasons why people should be good." Discuss.

Jan 2011 Asks us to link relativism to abortion issues and discuss whether the outcome is immoral.

Jan 2013 (a & b)

✓ Explain the concept of absolute morality.

✓ "Considering consequences is more important than following rules." Discuss.

▸ Absolute and objective

This link has not been examined up to and including May 2013 although Jan 2013 did ask us to explain generally the idea of absolute morality.

Possible future question (a & b)

★ Explain to what extent absolute ethical theories are also objective.

★ "Objective ethical theories mean that the truth applies everywhere, for all time." Discuss.

▸ Relative and subjective

This link has not been examined up to May 2014.

Possible future question (a & b)

★ Explain to what extent relative ethical theories are necessarily subjective.

★ "A relativist inevitably sees issues surrounding euthanasia as a subjective choice." Discuss.

▸ Deontological and teleological

May 2012 (part a & b)

✓ Explain the difference between deontological and teleological theories.

✓ "The end never justifies the means." Discuss

Jan 2013 (part b)

✓ "Considering consequences is more important than following rules." Discuss

Possible future questions (a & b)

★ Explain the difference between subjective and objective theories of ethics.

★ "Only objective theories of ethics are useful when considering issues surrounding abortion." Discuss

★ Explain how an ethical theory you have studied may be considered subjective.

★ "Subjective theories of ethics are of no use in solving ethical dilemmas." Discuss

Ethical theories: Natural law

▸ **Link Aquinas' theory to Aristotle's idea of Natural Purpose**

Possible future question (a & b)

★ Explain how Aquinas' Natural Law theory uses Aristotle's idea of Natural Human Purpose

★ "Natural Law theory has an unrealistic view of human nature." Discuss.

▸ **Consider Aquinas' view of purpose and eudaimonia (excellence or perfection)**

Possible future question (a & b)

★ Explain how Aquinas' Natural Law theory links natural purpose to eudaimonia

★ "Eudaimonia is inevitably subjective." Discuss

▸ **Examine how Natural law theory is linked to human reason**

Jan 2012 (a & b)

✓ Explain how Natural Law theory can be used to decide the right moral action.

✓ To what extent is Natural Law the best approach to ethical decision-making?

Possible future question (a & b)

★ Explain how Natural Law theory could be described as reasonable.

★ "Natural Law theory leads to unreasonable outcomes." Discuss.

▸ **Thoroughly understand and explain primary and secondary precepts**

Possible future question (a & b)

★ Explain the difference between primary and secondary precepts in Natural Law.

★ "Primary precepts are absolute, but secondary precepts are relative." Discuss.

▸ **Consider each of these critically and assess their strengths and weaknesses**

Jan 2010 (a & b) and Jan 2013 (a & b) also linked Natural Law to embryo research

✓ Explain the strengths of Natural Law theory.

✓ To what extent would a follower of Natural Law accept embryo research.

May 2011 (a & b)

✓ Explain how the followers of Natural Law might approach the issues surrounding abortion.

✓ "Natural Law has no serious weaknesses." Discuss.

Possible future question (a & b)

★ Explain how Natural Law theory might address issues surrounding genetic engineering.

★ "Natural Law's strengths outweigh its weaknesses." Discuss.

Ethical theories: Kantian ethics

▸ **Consider the differences between the hypothetical and categorical imperatives**

Jan 2011 (part a)

✓ Explain Kant's argument for using the Categorical Imperative. (this is a slightly different question from "explain Kant's Categorical Imperative")

✓ "The universalisation of maxims by Kant cannot be defended." Discuss.

May 2011 (a & b)

✓ Explain the difference between the hypothetical and categorical imperative.

✓ How useful is the categorical imperative when applied to embryo research?

Possible future question (a & b)

★ Explain how Kant's Categorical Imperative may be described as absolute.

★ "Absolute imperatives lead to immoral outcomes." Discuss

▸ **Know about different ways of expressing the one Categorical Imperative**

Possible future question (a & b)

★ Explain two variations of Kant's Categorical Imperative.

★ "The Categorical Imperative is difficult to apply to issues surrounding abortion." Discuss.

▸ Know how to explain "universalisation of maxims"

Notice that there are two key terms here, **UNIVERSALISATION** (or universalisability as it's more usually called) and the idea of a maxim. It's worth considering what is meant by a **MAXIM**.

Jan 2011 (b)

✓ "The universalisation of maxims by Kant cannot be defended." Discuss.

Possible future question (a & b)

★ Explain how Kant establishes the universalisation of ethical maxims.

★ "Universalisable maxims must be absolute." Discuss

▸ Consider what duty might mean in the context of Kant's ethics

The word "duty" has never come up in an exam question, so we should expect it sometime.

May 2013 (a & b)

✓ Asks us to use examples to explain why Kant stresses "doing one's duty."

✓ Asks us to evaluate the importance of "doing one's duty."

Possible future question (a & b)

★ Explain what Kant meant by always doing our "duty for duty's sake."

★ "The idea of duty is over-restrictive." Discuss.

▶ Consider Kant's ideas of "moral law," "good will" and "summum bonum"

These are three technical terms which have not been used before in exam questions - so we might expect them.

Possible future questions (a & b)

★ Explain Kant's idea of the summum bonum.

★ "The motive of duty is incompatible with the end of the summum bonum." Discuss.

★ Explain what Kant meant by "the good will."

★ "Kant places motive above consequences." Discuss.

★ Explain how Kant establishes the idea of the moral law.

★ "Legalistic theories are of no use when considering issues surrounding abortion." Discuss.

Ethical theories: Utilitarianism

▸ Consider Bentham and Mill's versions of Utilitarianism

Jan 2012 (a & b)

- ✓ Explain the differences between the Utilitarianism of Bentham and Mill.
- ✓ "The Utilitarianism of Mill is superior in every way to that of Bentham." Discuss.

Jan 2013 (a)

- ✓ Explain how Mill's Utilitarianism might be used to decide the right course of action.

May 2013 (a & b)

- ✓ Asks us to explain the major forms of classical utilitarianism.
- ✓ Asks us to discuss whether utilitarian ethics is a good way for resolving moral dilemmas.

Possible future question (a & b)

- ★ Explain how Mill develops Bentham's idea of Utilitarianism. (Note: Jan 2013 asked us specifically about Mill's Utilitarianism)
- ★ "Mill's version of Utilitarianism is superior to Bentham's." Discuss.

▸ Compare and contrast the two theories

Jan 2012 (a & b)

- ✓ Explain the main differences between the Utilitarianism of Bentham and that of Mill.
- ✓ The Utilitarianism of Mill is superior in every way to that of Bentham." Discuss.

> ## Consider the hedonic calculus of Bentham, and Mill's qualitative pleasures, and the difference between Act and Rule Utilitarianism

Jan 2011 (a & b)

✓ Explain the difference between Act and Rule Utilitarianism.

✓ To what extent is Utilitarianism useful in making decisions about euthanasia?

Possible future questions (a & b)

★ Explain the difference between higher and lower pleasures in the Utilitarianism of Bentham and Mill

★ "The idea of pleasure is of no practical use when considering issues surrounding euthanasia." Discuss.

★ Explain how Bentham's hedonic calculus might be applied by a person considering an abortion.

★ "Teleological theories are superior to deontological theories when making practical decisions." Discuss.

> ## Consider the Preference Utilitarianism of Peter Singer

May 2011 (a & b)

✓ Explain the Preference Utilitarianism of Peter Singer.

✓ To what extent is Preference Utilitarianism the best form of Utilitarianism?

Possible future question (a & b)

★ Explain how a Preference Utilitarian might approach issues surrounding abortion.

★ "Preference Utilitarianism leads to immoral outcomes." Discuss

▶ Critical assessment and strengths and weaknesses

Jan 2010 (part a)

✓ Explain how Utilitarians approach the issues of war.

Jan 2012 (part b)

✓ "The Utilitarianism of Mill is superior in every way to that of Bentham." Discuss.

Jan 2013 (b)

✓ Assess the extent to which Utilitarianism is a reliable method of making decisions about abortion.

Ethical theories: Religious ethics

▸ **Consider the principles of our chosen religion and how followers make decisions**

Jan 2011 (a & b)

✓ Explain how a follower of any religion makes ethical decisions.

✓ "Religion and morality are separate." Discuss.

May 2013 (a & b)

✓ Asks us to explain how religious ethics might approach issues of infertility.

✓ Asks us to discuss whether the right to a child is absolute.

▸ **Understand how morality and religion are or are not linked**

Jan 2011 (a & b as above)

✓ Explain how a follower of any religion makes ethical decisions.

✓ "Morality and religion are separate." Discuss.

▸ **Consider how far morality depends on God, as in Divine Command Theory**

Possible future questions (a & b)

★ Explain how far morality depends on God of a religion you have studied.

★ "Morality must depend on reason, not God." Discuss.

★ Explain how the followers of religion you have studied take ethical decisions.

★ "Religious ethics must originate in God's commands." Discuss.

Links the idea of religious ethics to the concepts of absolute and relative ethics

Possible future question (a & b)

★ Explain whether the ethics of a religion you have studied should be described as absolute or relative.

★ "Religious Ethics can lead to immoral outcomes." Discuss.

▸ **Consider how ethical theories (we assume the specification means theories such as such as Natural Law, Kantian ethics) can be considered "religious"**

For example, I interpret this as asking is Kant's theory a religious ethical theory or not? Is Natural Law by definition "religious?"

Possible future question (a & b)

★ Explain how we might describe a particular moral theory as "religious."

★ "All morality comes from God." Discuss.

▸ **Critical assessment and strengths and weaknesses**

Jan 2010 (a & b)

✓ Explain how the ethics of a religion you have studied might be applied to abortion.

✓ "Religious ethics fail to consider the consequences." Discuss.

June 2010 (a & b)

✓ Explain the ethical religious principles involved in war.

✓ "War should not be allowed under any circumstances." Discuss.

Jan 2012 (a & b)

✓ Explain the main ethical principles of a religion you have studied with regard to genetic engineering.

✓ "Religious ethics prevents progress in genetic engineering." Discuss.

May 2012 (a & b)

✓ Explain how the followers of a religion you have studied justify going to war.

✓ "Religious believers should be pacifist." Discuss.

Jan 2012 (a & b)

✓ Explain the main ethical principles of a religion you have studied with regard to genetic engineering.

✓ "Religious ethics prevents progress in genetic engineering." Discuss.

Possible future questions (a & b)

★ Explain the main ethical principles of a religion you have studied with regard to euthanasia.

★ "Religious ethics causes unnecessary suffering." Discuss.

★ Explain the main ethical principles of a religion you have studied with regard to the issues surrounding a right to a child.

★ "Children are the gift of God." Discuss.

★ Explain the major strengths of a religious ethic you have studied.

★ "The strengths of religious ethics outweigh their weaknesses." Discuss.

Applied ethics: Abortion - the right to a child

▸ **Consider the sanctity of life**

Possible future question (a & b)

★ Explain how the concept of the sanctity of life affects issues surrounding abortion.

★ "The foetus is a human person." Discuss.

▸ **Understand the concept of personhood**

Jan 2012 (part a)

✓ Explain how concepts of personhood influence ethical approaches to abortion.

▸ **Apply the idea of "right to life" to abortion**

Jan 2012 (part b)

✓ "The right to life is the most important factor when considering issues surrounding abortion." Discuss.

Possible part b question

★ "The foetus has a right to life." Discuss.

▸ **Examine issues around infertility and the idea of a "right to a child"**

Note, don't muddle up abortion and right to a child although they are in the same syllabus area. In June 2012 the examiner notes "some candidates struggled with the concept 'right to a child' and attempted responses which focused on the issue of abortion."

June 2010 (a & b)

✓ Explain how a follower of Kantian ethics might approach the issues surrounding the right to a child.

✓ "The right to a child is an absolute right." Discuss.

May 2012 (part a)

✓ Asks us in a part a. question to explain, in general terms, the issues surrounding a right to a child.

Possible part b question

★ "The right to a child is a meaningless concept." Discuss.

▸ **Determine whether a child is a gift or a right**

June 2010 (part b)

✓ "The right to a child is an absolute right." Discuss.

May 2012 (part b)

✓ 'A child is a gift not a right'. Discuss.

▸ **Apply the ethical theories of Kant, Utilitarianism, Natural Law and Religious Ethics to abortion and right to a child**

The syllabus suggests issues of personhood, rights and sanctity of life are three that should be considered).

Jan 2010 (part a)

✓ Explain how the ethics of a religion you have studied might be applied to abortion.

Jan 2011 (part a)

✓ Explain how a moral relativist might approach issues raised by abortion.

May 2011 (part a)

✓ Explain how a follower of Natural Law might approach the issues surrounding abortion.

Jan 2013 (b)

✓ Assess the extent to which Utilitarianism is a reliable method of making decisions about abortion.

Possible future question (a & b)

★ Explain how the follower of a religion (substitute a Kantian or Utilitarian here) might approach issues surrounding the right to a child.

★ "Children are the gift of God." Discuss.

Applied ethics: Euthanasia

▸ Apply 'Sanctity of Life' to euthanasia

May 2013 (part b)

✓ Asks us to weigh up whether the "sanctity of life" is the most important issue when considering euthanasia.

Possible future question (a & b)

★ Explain how a Natural Law theorist might argue for the sanctity of human life.

★ "Sanctity of life is more important than quality of life." Discuss.

▸ Apply quality of life to euthanasia

May 2012 (part b)

✓ "Quality of life is the most important factor when considering issues surrounding euthanasia." Discuss.

May 2013 (part a)

✓ Asks us to explain "quality of life" as applied to euthanasia.

▸ Apply right to life to euthanasia

Possible future question (part b)

★ "The right to life includes the right to choose your own death." Discuss.

★ "Passive euthanasia violates the right to life'. Discuss.

▸ **Link the approaches of the ethical theories of Kant, Natural law, Utilitarianism and Religious Ethics to euthanasia**

Jan 2011 (part b)

✓ To what extent is Utilitarianism a useful method of making decisions about euthanasia?

May 2012 (part a)

✓ Explain the moral issues surrounding euthanasia.

Applied ethics: Genetic engineering

▸ **Apply genetic engineering to humans, animals and embryos and understand the issues**

Jan 2010 (part b) and Jan 2013 (part a made this same link to embryos)

✓ To what extent could the followers of Natural law accept embryo research.

▸ **Link Kant, Natural Law, Utilitarianism and Religious Ethics to issues raised by genetic engineering**

Jan 2010 (part b)

✓ Asks us in part b to discuss whether the followers of Natural Law could accept embryo research (see above).

Jan 2013 (part a & b)

✓ Explain how a follower of Natural Law might respond to human embryo research.

✓ To what extent can human embryo research be justified?

Applied ethics: War and peace

▸ **Understand and apply Just War principles**

Jan 2013 (part a & b)

✓ Explain the purpose and principles of Just War theory.

✓ "Just War theory cannot be applied to modern warfare." Discuss.

Possible future (a & b)

★ Explain how a follower of a religion you have studied creates principles of Just War.

★ "War is never justified." Discuss

▸ **Understand theories of ethical and religious pacifism**

May 2011 (a & b)

✓ Explain the theories of ethical and religious pacifism.

✓ Assess the claim that killing in war is more justifiable than other types of killing.

May 2012 (a & b)

✓ Explain how followers of a religion you have studied justify war.

✓ "Religious followers should be pacifist." Discuss.

▸ **Discuss how Kant, Natural Law Theory, Utilitarianism and Religious Ethics might handle issues of war and peace**

Jan 2010 (a & b)

✓ Explain how Utilitarians approach issues of war.

✓ "Pacifism does more harm than good." Discuss.

June 2010 (a & b)

✓ Explain the ethical principles of a religion you have studied in relation to war.

✓ "War should not be allowed even as a last resort." Discuss.

Possible future question (a & b)

★ Explain how a Kantian might justify going to war.

★ "There can be no hard and fast rules about going to war." Discuss.

Possible future question (a & b)

★ Explain how followers of a religion you have studied handle issues of war and peace.

★ "A Just War must produce a Just peace." Discuss.

A2 ETHICS (OCR G582)

The A2 specification includes the theories studied in the AS syllabus. On three out of 24 questions set the examiner has specifically mentioned one of these theories: Jan 2010 (Utilitarianism linked to the environment), June 2012 (Religious Ethics and Business), and Jan 2011 (Natural Law and Sex). So we need to revise these old theories and relate them particularly to issues in business and environmental ethics, and issues in sexual ethics. In the analysis below, we examine which areas of the syllabus have been examined on up to June 2012, and the questions we might expect in the future are indicated by a star. All questions are worth **35 marks**.

Ethical topics and theories: Meta-ethics

▸ **Examine how ethical language (good, bad, right, wrong) is used**

June 2013

✓ Asks us to assess whether the word 'good' has real meaning.

Possible future question

★ "The meaning of 'good' varies from ethical theory to ethical theory." Discuss.

▸ **Explore how meta-ethics is different from normative ethics**

Possible future question

★ "Meta-ethical theories are of no practical use." Discuss.

▸ **Examine the different approaches using terms such as cognitive, non-cognitive, naturalism, emotivism, prescriptivism and intuitionism.**

These then need to be applied to ethical statements

June 2011

✓ "Ethical statements are no more than expressions of emotion." Discuss.

Jan 2012

✓ "All ethical language is prescriptive." Discuss.

May 2012

✓ To what extent do moral statements have objective meaning? (The word "objective" is not in this syllabus but occurs in theory section of the AS syllabus)

Possible future questions

★ "Ethical language is essentially naturalistic." Discuss.

★ "All moral language is based on intuition." Discuss.

★ Critically assess whether all moral language is subjective.

▸ Assess the different theories critically

Jan 2010

✓ To what extent is ethical language meaningful?

June 2013

✓ Asks us to assess whether the word 'good' has real meaning.

Possible future question

★ Critically assess which meta-ethical theory is most useful in determining the meaning of ethical language.

Ethical topics: Free will and determinism

▶ **Examine three approaches: hard determinism, soft determinism and libertarianism**

Possible future question

★ Critically assess the libertarian approach to free will and moral responsibility.

▶ **Examine and understand the views of Darrow, Honderich, Hume and Locke**

Possible future question

★ Critically assess Honderich's theory of determinism.

▶ **Look at religious aspects of free will and predestination**

Possible future question

★ "Free will is incompatible with predestination: therefore God cannot judge us." Discuss

▶ **Look at different influences, such as genes, psychology, environment and social conditioning for moral choices**

Jan 2011

✓ "Our ethical decisions are merely the result of social conditioning." Discuss.

Possible future question

★ "Human beings are a product of genes and environment. Therefore there can be no moral responsibility." Discuss.

- **Look at the implications of genes, psychology, environment and social conditioning for moral responsibility**

  June 2013

  ✓ Asks us to consider whether freedom is necessary in order to make an ethical choice.

- **Examine the links between free will, determinism and moral responsibility**

  June 2010

  ✓ Critically assess the claim that people are free to make moral choices.

  May 2011

  ✓ Critically assess the view that we are not responsible for our actions.

- **Discuss all these elements critically**

  Jan 2012

  ✓ Critically assess the claim that free will and determinism are compatible.

  Possible future questions

  ★ "If hard determinism is true there can be no moral responsibility." Discuss.

  ★ Critically evaluate the hard determinist (or libertarian or compatibilist) theory of free will.

Ethical theories: Nature and role of conscience

▸ **Differentiate between the ideas of conscience as God-given, innate and produced by reason as an "inner voice," or instilled by society, parents and authority figures**

Jan 2011

✓ Critically assess whether conscience is the voice of reason.

The examiner commented on students answers: "Some candidates who discussed Aquinas did not seem clear about his ideas on conscience and did not refer to synderesis, conscientia or recta ratio. There also tended to be little distinction between the views of Butler or Newman," (Jan 2011 report).

May 2012

✓ This question linked Butler's theory to the idea of Innateness.

Possible future questions

★ "Conscience is a product of our upbringing and environment, and so is an unreliable authority for moral decisions." Discuss.

★ Critically assess the view that conscience is the voice of God.

▸ **Consider whether conscience is a reliable guide to moral decision-making**

Jan 2010

✓ Assess the view that conscience need not always be obeyed.

Jan 2012

✓ "For moral issues surrounding sex the demands of conscience override other ethical considerations." Discuss.

Jan 2013

✓ Critically assess the claim that conscience is a reliable guide to ethical decision-making.

▸ **Consider specific views of: Augustine, Aquinas, Butler, Newman, Freud, Fromm and Piaget**

Possible future questions

★ Critically assess the view that Freudian theories of conscience undermine ideas of free will.

★ Compare and evaluate the views of Fromm and Freud on the origins of conscience.

Ethical topics: Virtue ethics

▸ **Examine the principles of Virtue Ethics starting with Aristotle**

Jan 2012

✓ To what extent do modern versions of Virtue Ethics address the weaknesses of Aristotle's teaching?

Possible future question

★ "Aristotelean Virtue Ethics is superior to modern approaches." Discuss.

▸ **Understand what it means to call Virtue Ethics "agent-centred"**

Possible future question

★ Critically assess agent-centred moral theories against law-based theories as a guide to practical decision-making.

▸ **Understand the concepts of eudaimonia and the Golden Mean**

Possible future question

★ "The goal of eudaimonia gives the clearest basis for determining moral goodness." Discuss.

- **Examine the importance of practising the virtues and following virtuous people**

  June 2011

  ✓ To what extent is Virtue Ethics useful in making decisions surrounding extra-marital sex?

  Jan 2013

  ✓ "Following thee example of virtuous people is the most useful aspect of Virtue Ethics." Discuss.

  June 2013

  ✓ "Businesses are completely incompatible with Virtue Ethics." Discuss.

(This question is also strangely worded as surely it is business practices which may be incompatible with Virtue Ethics, or perhaps the practices of business people?)

- **Compare Aristotle with more modern theories (but doesn't mention any one specifically)**

  Jan 2012

  ✓ To what extent does modern Virtue Ethics address the weaknesses of Aristotle's teaching on virtue?

(Note: there are many modern Virtue Ethicists from Robert Louden to Philippa Foot to Alasdair MacIntyre. Both teachers and students need to be clear which one or ones they are talking about as they don't necessarily say the same thing).

Applied ethics: Environmental and business

▶ **Ask how we as humans should relate to the environment**

Possible future question

★ "We have a duty to protect the environment." Discuss.

▶ **Understand secular approaches (the Gaia hypothesis)**

Possible future question

★ "The Gaia hypothesis is the only theory that gives moral significance to the environment." Discuss.

▶ **Examine issues in business and mentions two relationships - with consumers and employees**

Jan 2013

✓ Critically assess the view that businesses have a moral duty to put their consumers first.

Possible future question

★ "Business puts profit before people and so lacks an ethical basis for decisions." Discuss.

▶ **Understand the relationship between business and the environment and business and the idea of globalisation**

Jan 2011

✓ "The environment suffers because business has no ethics." Discuss.

The examiner commented on student answers: "Many gave emotive responses, writing about the importance of the environment without questioning the role of business or being able to provide any evidence for their responses," (Jan 2011 report).

Possible future question

★ "Ethical theories cannot guide business effectively in making decisions on issues surrounding globalisation." Discuss.

▸ **Apply the different theories (secular and religious, including those studied at AS level) to issues raised by environmental and business ethics**

Jan 2010

✓ "Utilitarianism is not the best approach to environmental issues." Discuss.

June 2010

✓ Assess the usefulness of Religious Ethics as an ethical approach to business. (This is one of three occasions out of 24 questions set between 2010 and 2013 where an ethical theory from the **AS SYLLABUS** is mentioned).

✓ A second one is the question above linking Utilitarianism to the environment.

June 2012

✓ To what extent are ethical theories helpful when considering ethical business practice?

June 2012

✓ "There is no moral imperative to care for the environment." Discuss.

In June 2012 and again in June 2013 two questions have been asked from one section of the syllabus, Environment and Business Ethics.

June 2013

✓ Asks us to consider whether businesses are compatible with Virtue Ethics.

June 2013

✓ Asks us to assess whether religious teaching on the environment is compatible with Gaia theory.

Comment: the fact that the examiner set two questions from one broad section of the syllabus suggests that it is dangerous to leave any section our of the six major sections of the A2 OCR Ethics syllabus. Moreover, this may well be the section that is least well taught in this paper - although I realise if students drop one section they tend to drop Meta-ethics.

Possible future question

★ "Ethical theories cannot take into account issues raised by the environment because no theory considers morally significant those yet unborn." Discuss.

Applied ethics: Sexual ethics

▸ **Understand the issues surrounding pre-marital sex, extra-marital sex, contraception and homosexuality**

June 2010

✓ To what extent are ethical theories useful in considering issues surrounding homosexuality.

Jan 2011

✓ "Natural Law is the most reliable approach when considering the issues surrounding premarital sex." Discuss.

This is one of three questions out of 24 surveyed which specifically mentions an AS theory. The examiner commented on student answers: "Some candidates made good use of the phrase 'most reliable approach' and were able to posit a range of more reliable or less reliable approaches, with clear evaluation as to the reasons for these views."

Possible future questions

★ To what extent are ethical theories useful when considering issues surrounding contraception.

★ To what extent are ethical theories useful in considering issues surrounding extramarital sex.

★ "Virtue Ethics is the best approach to issues surrounding sex and relationships." Discuss.

> ## Review and analyse how the theories we have studied at AS level and A2 might help us apply ethical principles to the issues raised by the previous point

Jan 2010

✓ "Some ethical theories are more useful than others in making decisions about sexual issues." Discuss.

Note: you are expected to know AS theories plus Virtue Ethics for this question - selecting two and contrasting them might be the best approach.

May 2011

✓ To what extent is Virtue Ethics helpful when making decisions about extra-marital sex?

Jan 2012

✓ "For moral issues surrounding sex the demands of conscience override other ethical considerations'. Discuss.

Jan 2013

✓ Asks us to contrast and evaluate religious approaches to sexual ethics and secular approaches.

Possible future questions

★ "Ethical theories are of no practical use when considering issues raised by contraception." Discuss.

★ "The morality of homosexuality is a matter of personal opinion." Discuss.

What the Examiner Says

Every year the examiner produces a report on student answers available on the OCR website. It is possible to extract from these general principles what goes wrong when you write essays under exam conditions. Actually the same points are made over and over again, as if no-one ever reads the reports and if they do, fail to learn from them. I have summarised here the main points the examiner makes, and then I suggest twelve things to practise to try and eliminate these errors.

AS ETHICS

Answer the question

It sounds an obvious point, but nearly every year the examiner complains that students are deviating off the question, either because they have learned a pre-prepared answer, or because they have more knowledge on another (perhaps related) area and so feel compelled to prove it.

Enormous efforts are made for little credit as this comment in January 2011 indicates:

> "An examination at this level is not primarily a test of what candidates know, but rather of how well they can respond to the question. Some candidates wrote at enormous length, covering every theory they could remember, but often without demonstrating how these might be remotely relevant."

As another example, here's a comment praising relevance from a recent report:

"Good candidates kept the question in mind throughout," (Jan 2012 AS Ethics Q4b)

You will not achieve an A grade if you don't answer the exact question set.

When you go into an exam, take a highlighter pen and highlight the key words and phrases. Hopefully, if you study this book carefully, you will understand what sort of command words (like 'Explain") to expect, and indeed, what kind of questions, as the examiner tends to repeat key phrases in different questions. A comment like the one below is fairly typical:

"Generally, candidates fared well provided they answered the question which had been set and not the one they hoped would be set. Candidates need to be reminded to read the question and then answer the question." (June 2012)

▸ **Practise: making a reference to the question in every paragraph you write**

▸ **Know your key terms throughly**

In a previous chapter I listed the technical vocabulary in different areas of the syllabus. This creates a minimal list of technical terms you must thoroughly understand and know. There is no excuse for entering an exam in a state of muddle over the distinction between a priori and a posteriori. Here is a comment from a recent examiner's reports.

> *"Unfortunately, there are still candidates who attempt this examination with insecure knowledge of basic philosophical concepts and terminology. Many remain unaware of the correct meaning of terms such as 'empirical', 'logical ', 'refute', 'metaphysical', 'a priori' or 'a posteriori'. Especially common errors were 'analytical' for 'analytic' – especially and 'scientifical' for 'scientific'. This subject presupposes familiarity with basic philosophical notions and some candidates have paid too little attention to these."* (AS, June 2012)

▸ **Practise: learning key definitions off by heart**

▸ **Reflect, don't just memorise**

> *"Some candidates appeared to have attempted to learn theories, leading to less successful responses: more able responses showed evidence of reflection on theories, with the best showing the benefits of original thought. It cannot be too often stressed that examiners – and the nature of the subject – expect candidates to demonstrate that they have considered and reflected on ideas and not merely learned them."* (AS, Jan 2012).

How do we "reflect on theories?" My argument in this book is that we reflect on theories by not just learning key points off by heart, but also by understanding (and being prepared to challenge) key **ASSUMPTIONS** the theory makes and reflecting carefully on the **WORLDVIEW** the theory comes out of. We then practise applying the key **PRINCIPLES** suggested by a theory to a particular issue (preferably using our own examples to ground the explanation).

▸ **Practise: reflective writing by peer group comparison and using examples of good practice on the website**

▸ **Show higher order skills**

> *"Despite good AO1 performance, AO2 skills were often lacking. It continues to be the characteristic of many candidates to believe that just because a number of philosophers have criticised a theory, it must be wrong, and when evaluating a question, you simply need to count the philosophers who make points on each side of the argument and see which side has more in it,"* (June 2012 examiners' report).

What are these AO1 and AO2 skills? In general terms these "descriptors" as they are called can be expressed thus for AS and A2 (at A2 the whole essay is assessed according to these).

AO1: In part a of AS questions you must select and demonstrate clearly relevant knowledge and understanding through the use of evidence, examples and correct language and terminology appropriate to Ethics and Philosophy of Religion.

For top marks (25 of the 35 marks are awarded for AO1 criteria at AS, 21 out of 35 at A2) you will need:

1. A very high level of ability to select and deploy relevant information;

2. Accurate use of technical terms;

3. A well-structured answer.

AO2: In part b of AS questions you must sustain a critical line of argument and justify a point of view.

For top marks (10 marks for AO2 criteria awarded out of 35 at AS, 14 marks awarded for these AO2 skills out of 35 at A2) you must:

1. Comprehend the demands of the question;

2. Use a wide range of evidence;

3. Show understanding and critical analysis of different viewpoints.

▸ **Practise: reading the list of AO2 skills before you start your essay, and re-read after you've finished**

▸ **Argue, don't assert**

It's worth reflecting long and hard on the longer quotes from examiner's reports below:

> *"A statement of a viewpoint is not an argument, and argument by assertion is inappropriate in philosophical writing. Many responses simply presented alternative viewpoints but made no attempt to use these to work to their own conclusions. Candidates would benefit from thinking through the implications of the descriptors in the published levels of response used for marking – these are invaluable for explaining precisely those abilities rewarded by examiners." (Jan 2012, AS)*

> *"It is important that candidates engage with arguments: examiners seek evidence that views have been thoughtfully*

considered. A list of the arguments of different philosophers does not become a considered argument simply because 'however' is occasionally inserted into a narrative account." (June 2012, AS)

▸ **Practise: constructing arguments using the thesis - argument - conclusion model described in my book: "How to Write Ethics Essays," (pushmepress.com, 2014).**

▸ **Illustrate with examples**

"Good marks were awarded for candidates who were able to demonstrate control of the material as well as being able to give examples from the biblical text to support their explanations." (June 2012 Q2a)

But make sure the examples are fresh and relevant. "Some candidates continued to use dubious examples to support their explanations and many not even ethical ones, as well as the usual 'helping an old lady to cross the road' and the 'stealing to feed a starving family'," (Jan 2012 AS Ethics).

The examiner also made clear that examples are a good way of explaining an ethical theory irrespective of whether a specific application is mentioned in the exam question. For example, the May 2013 exam question linked Kantian ethics to the idea of duty. The examiner commented:

"Some candidates were able to give a number of examples to illustrate their response. Kant's own examples were given by a number of candidates to good effect, and some candidates

produced interesting responses which approached this question differently, by incorporating knowledge of Kant through specific examples. Some candidates had knowledge, but limited understanding, of Kant; this was evident in the lack of examples given and the fact that they simply wrote general responses focusing on the idea of doing one's duty without explaining how this might be achieved." (June 2013 AS Ethics)

▸ **Practise: finding film extracts, news stories or incidents in novels that illustrate ethical principles. Watch new films critically**

▸ **Produce an argument, not a list**

It is worth reflecting again on what constitutes an argument. If you have difficulty knowing how to practise forming an argument, I give plenty of examples in my book "How to Write Ethics Essays," (pushmepress.com, 2014). Weaker candidates simply list points, rather than integrate them into a line of reasoning. A grade candidates argue and explain points, showing how they link to assumptions and worldviews. Here's a comment that confirms this problem:

"Weaker candidates tended to write as much as they knew without focusing on command words such as 'explain'. Some candidates continued to use dubious examples to support their explanations and many not even ethical ones, as well as the usual 'helping an old lady to cross the road' and the 'stealing to feed a starving family'," (June 2012 AS Ethics)

And on Utilitarianism, there is this comment:

"Weaker responses simply described the differences (between Act and Rule Utilitarianism) without any explanation of the reasons behind them," *(Jan 2012 AS Ethics Q1a).*

▸ **Practise: producing argument plans which sketch out counter-arguments and objections, like the Socratic method**

▸ **Be aware of the various issues (and applications) within a topic**

The examiner stressed in the 2010 June report that "candidates must learn how to apply ethical theories to practical ethical issues. Many candidates do not know how to do so and therefore cannot access the higher marks."

"Unfortunately, many candidates seemed to have only a very basic knowledge of what genetic engineering involved. Many candidates only focused on human genetic engineering without mentioning animals or plants. Some candidates focused entirely on IVF treatment without discussing issues such as genetic selection or testing for disease, resulting in a limited viewpoint." (Jan 2012 AS Ethics Q2b)

An example of an AS Ethics candidate praised highly by the examiner involves using an entirely correct, but unusual argument in answer to a question (Jan 2012 Q4) on Natural Law: "One candidate wrote an excellent response showing that Natural Law can be both absolute and relative." (Jan 2012 report on AS Ethics).

- ▶ Practise: working out the issues surrounding abortion, etc, and then applying moral theories to these issues. Try to extract principles from theories
- ▶ Find out about modern interpretations

Even when the syllabus doesn't mention them, the examiner clearly likes original, up-to-date comments about the theories set at AS. One example, which slightly surprised me because it seems to depart from the syllabus, is this comment about modern interpretations of Natural Law theory: "Many were able to make reference to more modern forms of Natural Law theory as found in Proportionalism. Key features such as the concept of telos, eudaimonia, the Primary and Secondary Precepts, apparent and actual goods and intentions behind actions were often highlighted," (Jan 2012 AS Ethics Q4a). When I read this it reminded me that I had never taught Bernard Hoose's theory of Proportionalism.

I was encouraged by this comment. The examiner is saying "don't read the syllabus over-narrowly." Why not use Christine Korsgaard (a modern Kantian) or Richard Hare (a twentieth century Utilitarian) to help reflect on these two theories?

- ▶ Practise: finding modern scholars who represent different viewpoints on old questions or theories
- ▶ **Consult the website for extracts listed by section**

A2 ETHICS

The June 2013 examiner's report for A2 Ethics praised the fact that fewer candidates were producing lists of points and were generally analysing the questions a little more effectively than in past years. However, two general points were made which I discuss below: candidates tend not to relate different parts of the syllabus to each other very effectively (for example, religious teachings to the environment or Kantian ethics to business practices). And candidates need to understand that to state a view is not the same as analysing a view: "candidates should be encouraged to do more than simply state views. 'Engagement with the material' is a key skill here as can be seen from the descriptors for Level 5 in AO1."

▸ **Lack of knowledge of key terms affects quality of answers**

The examiner's report repeatedly makes the same point at A2 as at AS, that key terms are not properly understood. For example: "A particular problem for many was inadequate grasp of the grammar of philosophy, with terms such as 'prove' used as a synonym for 'argue'. Some would say of each thinker cited that he had 'proved' his view, even when it was controversial or opposed by other alleged 'proofs'; 'refute' used to mean 'deny'; a priori often mistakenly used for 'innate'; a posteriori, 'analytic' and 'metaphysical' were commonly misunderstood." (Jan 2012, A2 report).

▸ **Practise: writing full definitions of key terms on index cards and learn them**

▸ **Integrate different parts of the syllabus**

Students tend to see the syllabus as a set of blocks unrelated to each other. However, the syllabus should be seen as one whole where every part is related (as mentioned in my preliminary comments above). Exam questions may for example, connect free will with conscience or business ethics with Kantian concepts of duty. A comment in June 2013 makes this clear:

> "Centres are encouraged to assist students in focusing on being able to make connections between different parts of the specification eg Business Ethics and Virtue Ethics or to make connections within one part eg Gaia hypothesis and religious approaches to environmental issues." (A2 report June 2013)

▸ **Write critical analysis**

Sometimes the examiner praises high quality candidates who go way beyond the syllabus with their analysis. One example is a question on Meta-ethics in the January 2012 exam, asking whether ethical language is necessarily prescriptive: "Some very good candidates used the ideas of Mackie and Charles Pigden using error theory to argue that there are no moral facts so prescriptivism is wrong and we can only use ethical language in an agreed social contract which makes it convenient for use to prescribe certain moral actions as right and wrong," (Jan 2012 A2 Ethics Q1).

▸ **Practise: writing under timed conditions taking past questions (and looking at the mark schemes available on the OCR site) and then trying my possible future questions in Chapter 4**

▶ **Read the original sources and engage with them**

Original sources are indicated in the specification. It is important to read these carefully and understand them for yourself, and not rely on text-book interpretations. The June 2013 report praises the evidence of fewer candidates producing lists of points. But note carefully the comment about "engaging with the material" - you are expected to show a critical and personal response to what scholars argue.

> *"Overall, it was pleasing to note that there seemed to be less of the "list approach" in responses whereby the views of each and every scholar were stated. However, candidates should be encouraged to do more than simply state views. 'Engagement with the material' is a key skill here as can be seen from the descriptors for Level 5 in AO1. It is important that candidates directly relate the views of different scholars to the question and analyse the material." (A2 Ethics June 2013)*

▶ **Practise: extracting your own quotes from original sources or scholars' views, and taking notes which map the arguments. Then give your own response**

▶ **Don't tack your evaluation on at the end**

The examiner has encouraged us to separate analysis and evaluation at AS level (part a is always analysis and part b evaluation) and now we are criticised for tacking evaluation on at the end. The only way to learn how to integrate the two effectively is to read good examples and then try to copy their style. This comes with practice. How to construct such essays, and the language to use, is dealt with in my book "How to Write Ethics Essays" (PushMe Press, 2014).

"Many candidates were able to attempt to analyse and evaluate elements within the main argument rather than tacked on as a paragraph at the end of their response," (Jan 2012 A2 Ethics).

▶ **Practise: taking a contrary position to a philosopher's view and producing summary sheets of strengths and weaknesses of different viewpoints**

But be very careful not to write your answer as a list of points. Always go through the question carefully highlighting key words and then relate your answer to the exact question set. An answer that never explicitly discusses the question in front of you isn't usually a good answer as it is too easy to fail to notice (or fail to discuss adequately) one key word in the question. Even if you are not completely sure you understand that key word, you should still discuss its possible meaning and present your own interpretation.

Lightning Source UK Ltd.
Milton Keynes UK
UKOW03f1556140214

226487UK00001B/1/P